Little Joe
"Be good and go where you are led"

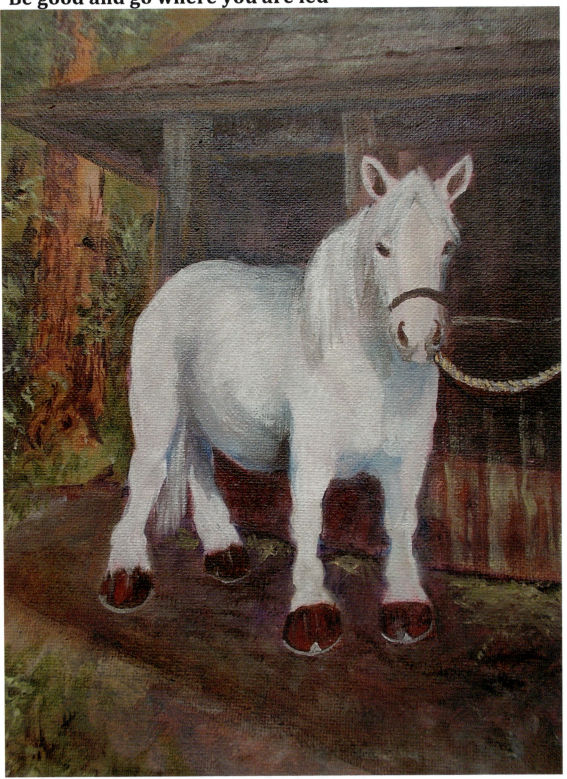

Written and Illustrated by Marty Pena

Dedication

For

Little Joe,
Zena,
And Duke

"The crew" at Mystic Seaport

With Much Love,
MARTY PEÑA

Joe soon realized he was not like the other horses.

Little Joe's Beginning

Little Joe was born on an Amish Farm. Joe soon realized he was not like the other horses. The horses were all Percherons, just like the farmers were all Amish. However, as all the colts grew, he noticed everyone else was taller than him. The farmers noticed too.

They also noticed his unusually big front feet; his short legs and big lop ears. They would laugh and make jokes,

"Look at him. He looks like he has his father's boots on!"

"What about those ears? He must be related to a bunny rabbit!"

When the colts played tag in the pasture Joe always got caught. He just wasn't as fast as the other horses.

The other colts grew taller and taller but Joe only grew wider. His legs did not grow to match his large Percheron draft horse body. His rather large ears had very sensitive hearing and the farmers' jokes hurt his feelings.

"Be good and go where you are led"

Motherly Advice

"Don't worry Joe. You are good-natured and sweet and that is better than being fast or tall. You are as strong as the other colts, both inside and out. In life it's best to be good and go where you are led." Joe's mother told him,

Joe did not know what she meant by all that but he supposed she was right. She was his mom after all and she would never steer him wrong.

Soon it was time for the young horses' training. They were taught to wear harnesses for pulling. They pulled big logs from the woods for making new barns, and large wagons full of hay; they also learned how to pull plows through the earth so the farmers could plant their crops.

All the colts grew very strong, as Percherons should be. Joe was feeling good about the work he was doing and his mother was proud. He did not even mind the occasional jokes about his big feet or floppy ears.

Then came the day when each colt was picked to be in a team. A pulling team has to be matched in every physical way. They have to be the same height and weight so they can work well together.

Sadly there was no match for Little Joe. He felt left out and sad. He could not even talk to his mom. He ran to the far corner of the pasture and hid behind a tree. He was the only horse not picked to be in a team.

The teams left for different farms. Soon after, Joe's mom was taken away to a different farm too. Poor Joe was left all alone. He thought that's fine, he did not want to talk or play with anyone anyway.

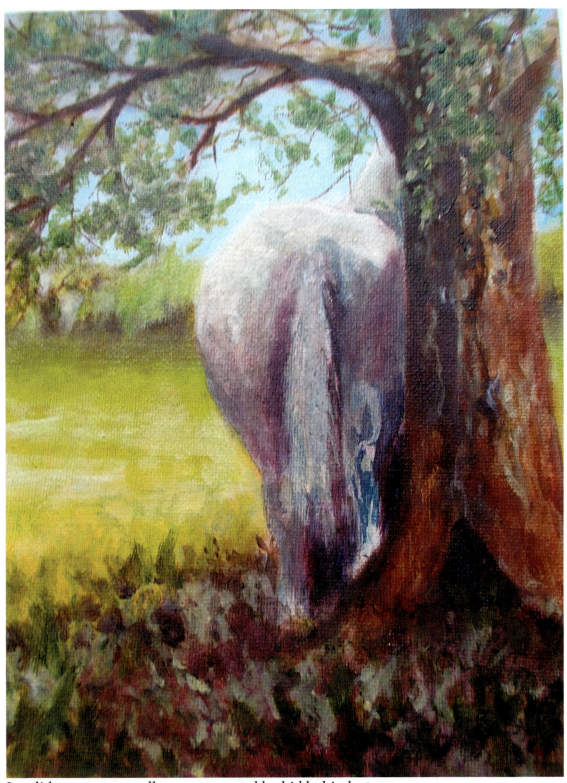
Joe did not want to talk to anyone and he hid behind a tree.

John

Before long a very old farmer came to get a look at Little Joe. The old man decided to take Joe to his farm. It was a very small farm. He was a kind man and he did not move very fast either because of his age.

Joe was glad to have been picked for something. Joe worked hard for the old farmer and he thought the farmer was pleased, but after few planting seasons another man came to look at Joe. The new man asked the old farmer,

"Why do you want to sell him?"

"Sell?" That was a new word for Joe, and he was not sure he liked it.

The farmer said,

"Little Joe is as good natured horse as I've ever owned. He is very strong but he is just too slow. I can't get all my fields planted on time."

"Joe is very strong but he is just too slow."

There it was again, Joe's short legs with big feet made him slow and just like that Joe was SOLD!

The new man's name was John and he had a big truck and trailer. Joe had never been in a trailer before but he walked right on. He remembered his mother's words that it is best to be good and go where you are led.

He was a little scared about being sold. John closed the trailer doors. Joe could still see through the slats of the trailer and he watched the little farm disappear as the truck and trailer rolled away.

Joe wondered where they were going and would he ever be part of a team? He rode in the trailer a long time, the sun went down and he could not see anything anymore except for the lights from the loud trucks and cars on the highway.

Joe was getting sleepy. For once Joe was grateful for his very big feet because they kept him very steady inside the swaying trailer. All horses can sleep standing up, it's a talent they have. However, Joe was not sure his long legged relatives would be able to sleep easily standing in a moving trailer. He turned his big ears back against his thick mane and blocked out the sounds of the highway, before long he was fast asleep.

Joe remembered his mother's words that is was best to be good and go where you are led.

Joe's new home

Joe did not know how long he was asleep but the next thing he knew the trailer had stopped and he saw the man named John opening the doors. John untied Joe's halter and led him out. He blinked his eyes, it was daylight, and he had been traveling in the trailer all night.

Little Joe looked around. There were lots of horses and he heard lots of whinnies. He whinnied back because he thought it was the polite thing to do. He saw many carriages of all shapes and sizes but no plows! He did not see any fields with crops either. He thought, what kind of farm is this? Joe was a bit nervous.

John put Joe in a small paddock will a big pile of hay and some fresh water. Joe pawed the ground, should he have a good roll in the dirt first or go straight to the hay? His tummy growled reminding him he was hungry. Hay now roll later he decided.

Joe could not help but notice his new neighbor a very tall and handsome Percheron savoring his own pile of hay. After John walked away toward his house, Joe's new neighbor spoke up.

"Hey kid, long trip?"

"I think so, I fell asleep."

"What's your name?"

"Little Joe"

"My name is Duke. You from Amish country?"

"Yes, I was born there. How did you know?" said Joe.

"I was born there too. Most of us were, then one day, John showed up and it was good bye plows!" Duke said with a big smile.

"I wasn't very good at plowing, the farmer said I was too slow, then he SOLD me! I thought he liked me." Joe said sadly.

"Cheer up Kid! That was your Lucky Day; there are no plows here! You won't find any horse here that misses that job."

"Hey kid, long trip?"

Duke

Little Joe soon found out that Duke was a very good listener. Before long, Joe told Duke his whole life story. The truth was Joe's life story, at that point, was not that long or that interesting.

"What kind of work do they do here, Duke?" Joe finally asked.

"We pull all kinds of wagons and carriages for all kind human events. We pull wagons for parades, parties and marriage proposals. We pull special fancy carriages to their happy weddings. We pull hearses or caissons to their sad funerals.

We even work on movie sets pulling all the different carriages. Why, I am known as somewhat of a movie star myself. The one thing we don't do here is pull any more plows!" Duke smiled.

Joe stood quietly for a moment and thought.

"I hope I can fit in here, Duke."

"Don't worry kid, I hear John is planning on having you work at the seaport with Zena and me."

"What's the seaport? And who is Zena?" Joe asked.

Duke nickered a little chuckle. He casually pointed with his nose, pretending to chase a fly, and then he added in a whisper.

"Zena is that good looking filly over there, who hasn't stopped looking at you since walked off that trailer."

Joe tried to be cool and steal a look at Zena. She was BEAUTIFUL! Joe also thought Zena did not look that much taller than him although she had gorgeous long legs.

Joe gave his thick mane a happy little shake, hoping Zena would notice his best feature. Things were definitely looking up.

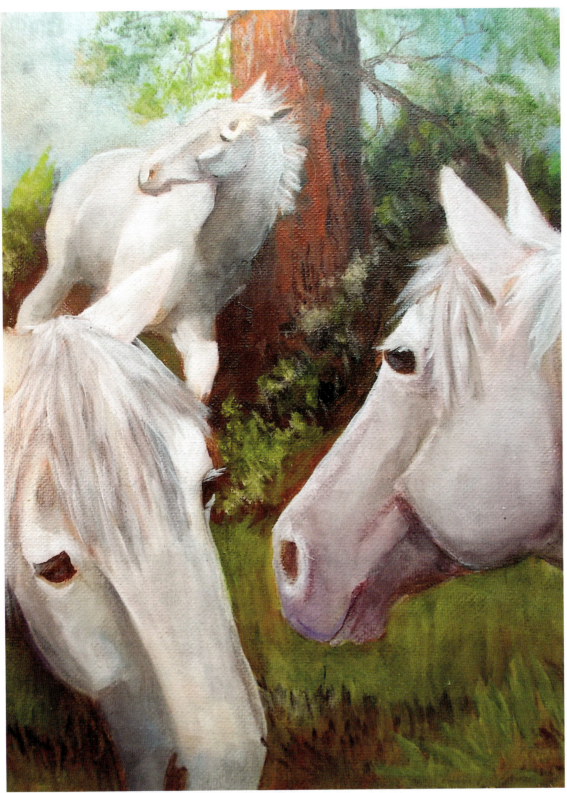
Zena and Loretta discuss Casper's silly habit.

Zena

Zena and a mare named Loretta were standing together. Near by Casper, Zena's goofy younger brother was busy itching his mane on a tree. Casper and Loretta were teammates.

"I don't know why he does that. It makes his mane all short like a crew cut." Loretta rolled her eyes.

"He's YOUR team mate Loretta." Zena replied.

"He's YOUR brother."

"Don't remind me."

"So, are you going to stand there staring at the new guy all day Zena?" teased Loretta.

"I'm not staring, Loretta. I just haven't finished my breakfast hay yet."

"Sure! Good thing you have that big bushy forelock to hide behind!" Loretta nickered.

"Oh stop! You were looking at the new horse just as much as I was."

"I was just checking to see if he looked like 'seaport material'."
Loretta smirked. "He is kind of cute. He could be YOUR new teammate!"

The two mares gave each other some playful shoves, squealed, kicked up their heals and cantered off.

"Come on let's head out to the big pasture, Loretta."

"Wait for me!" Casper whinnied and cantered off behind.

New work

Over the next few weeks, John would harness Joe, hitch him to different carriages and drive him around the farm and down different roads. Joe pulled them all with ease but not with a lot of speed.

John is a cheerful man and Joe liked working for him. They finished each drive and John would give Joe a hearty pat on his neck and tell him what a good boy he was.

Then one day John joked.

"You're a good boy Little Joe but we should call you Slow Joe."

"Uh Oh!" thought Joe, *"the last time I heard those words I was SOLD!"*

Then John added,

"I think you will work well for the seaport job. You don't need to be fast to work there. You'll give the tour guides plenty of time to point out the sights there."

"Phew!" Joe let out a big long sigh. "I have a job."

Joe had no idea what the job was like but he was not going to be sold and that was a big relief!

Tongue-tied

The next day the horses left for the seaport. Joe and Duke were put on the trailer first. Joe had lots of questions for Duke.

"Is it a long ride to the seaport? What is a seaport? What kind of carriages do we have to pull? Is it hard work? Are there fields? Are there any plows? Do we...."

"SLOW DOWN! KID! Give a horse a chance to answer." Duke said.

"Sorry, Duke, I guess I'm a little excited. That's the first time in my life anyone has ever told me to slow down."

Duke chuckled.

"I already told you. There are no plows on the jobs here. Why, when I first started at the seaport many years ago I could not stop smiling for weeks. It is easy work and the seaport staff always sneak us extra carrots and apples."

Joe liked the idea of extra treats. He loved carrots and apples.

Duke continued to explain the work they were expected to do at the seaport.

"The summer is the busiest time, there are many vacationers visiting the seaport. For special event weekends, John puts two carriages on duty and two horses share the work."

Duke smiled.

"Though, most of the time each horse works one long day giving tours then has two days off!"

Joe was concerned,

"You mean we work Sundays on weekends? Oh, I don't know if the Amish would approve of that idea."

Duke snorted a big horselaugh.

"I'm not sure they would approve of the two days off either. They probably have a wise proverb about *'idle hooves being the devil's workshop.'*

Joe realized life was certainly going to be different here in his new home.
Just then Zena was loaded onto the trailer.

"Good morning Zena." said Duke.

"Good Morning, Duke"

Duke always the gentleman introduced Little Joe to Zena.

Joe wanted to be polite suddenly found he was tongue-tied. He had never been this close to Zena before. Joe could feel his nose turning pink. All he could manage to say was.

"Mmmmffffffffffgggg!!!"

Percherons originally carried Knights in Armor

The Ride to the Seaport

Fortunately, Duke kept the conversation going on the journey to the seaport. Zena was beautiful and Joe was afraid to try to say any thing else. He didn't want to make a burro out of himself again. He decided it would be best to practice his listening skills.

Duke was telling Joe about the seaport.

"It's what the humans call a living museum. A museum is a place where humans go to learn about their history. The seaport is like a tiny town of very old buildings and very old sailing ships. The best known ship is the Charles W Morgan, the last wooden whaling ship."

Joe nodded his head that he understood. At least he could do that without looking silly around the beautiful Zena.

Duke went on.

"Around here is different from the Amish country where you and I were born. Here all the people drive cars and trucks everywhere, so seeing a horse and carriage is a rare thing. Visitors come to the museum to learn about the country's history. At the museum we horses pull carriages and our drivers give tours so the museum visitors can learn about the buildings and decide where they want to go first."

Without thinking Joe said

"I see."

He must be more relaxed because that sounded like those words came out normal. He even thought he saw Zena smile.

"Duke, do Percherons have a history?"

"We sure do. Our ancestors originally came from France all the way across the great ocean. Our first purpose was to carry knights in armor in medieval times. We carried the knights to battle and jousting tournaments.

Later in history we were brought to America in sailing ships. We helped to build this country with our strong backs pulling plows and the pioneers' Conestoga wagons. Our ancestors graded the country's first roads and worked building the levies.

Of course our friends the mules helped along the way too. I'm the kind of horse that gives credit where it's due."

Joe realized Duke was very smart and wise.

"How did you learn so much history, Duke?"

"Oh. I tune in on interesting conversations at the museum. Most of the movies I've been in have been about human history. I'm a very good listener."

"I noticed."

Joe tossed his head up and down in agreement.

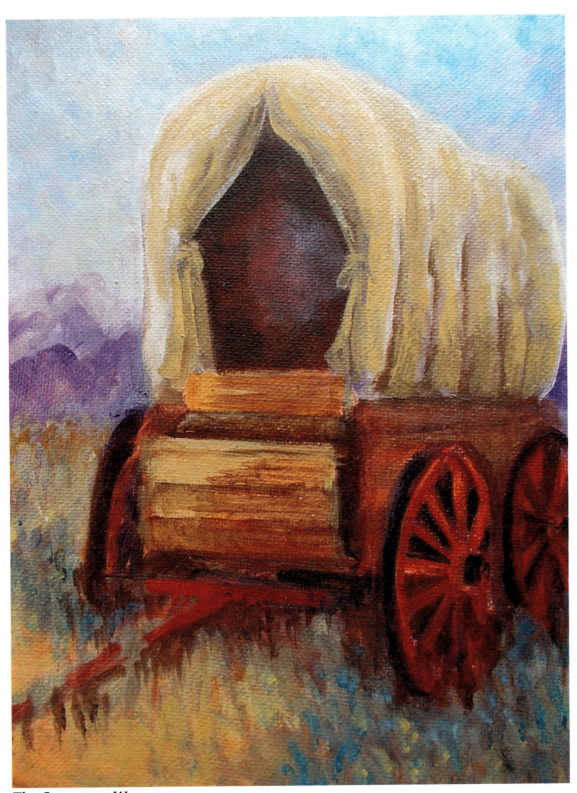

The Conestoga Wagon

The Seaport

"Is it a long ride to the seaport?" Asked Joe.

Duke looked out the window. "No, in fact we just turned off the highway, we're slowing down. We'll be there soon."

Little Joe was excited. He could hardly wait to see the seaport.

The trailer made some slow tight turns, Joe steadied himself by placing his large feet farther apart, and then they came to a stop. Quick as could be, John opened up the doors. Zena was led out first, then Joe and finally Duke. Each horse was put in a stall. Then in a blink of an eye, John closed up the trailer and left!

"Wait!" Joe whinnied "Where's he going? Is he just going to leave us here?

"Relax. Eat your hay." Said Zena "He'll be back, he just has to take the truck and trailer out before the museum opens."

Joe could feel his nose turning pink again.

Then Duke spoke up,

"Welcome to the 1860's, Little Joe, before there were any automobiles. You see when the visitors come here, it's like they are stepping back in time. Back to a time when the horse and sailing ships were the only ways to travel"

Joe could see water and some sailing ships from his stall.

"Is that the ocean?" Joe asked.

Both Zena and Duke chuckled. Then Duke said,

"No, that's the Mystic River. It flows out into Long Island Sound then the ocean but you can't see the ocean from here."

Joe was a bit embarrassed about how much he did not know about the world. He could feel his nose turning pink again. He decided it best to bury it in his hay.

Joe could feel his nose turning pink again and decided to bury it in his hay.

The Depot Wagon

Before long John was back and with another lady named Anne. Joe found out that she and Duke had worked together for a very long time.

Anne got busy grooming Duke and John began brushing Joe. When both horses were clean, their harness was put on. Joe had not seen Duke in harness before. There was one word for that horse hitched to his carriage and it was "Elegant". No wonder Duke got picked to be in movies so often.

Duke and Anne left the stable. Joe noticed that there were more people walking into the seaport now. John was hitching Joe to a very old carriage called the depot wagon. John gave Joe a friendly pat.

"Ready Joe? We won't be taking on passengers right away. We're going to just drive around and let you get used to the place first."

Joe was relieved, "taking on passengers," sounded like a lot of responsibility. He could tell the seaport was much busier than the Amish farm he left behind.

The depot wagon was built in the 1860's and like most old things it makes a lot of creaks and squeaks as it rolls along. The wheels have metal rims, which make it extra noisy too. The seaport also has some spots where the road is made of broken up clamshells. Put those noises all together and you have a recipe for making a very spooky horse.

The unfamiliar noises of the old wagon did make Joe a little jumpy. He pranced and spooked at some things he had never seen before. For some reason, he found it very difficult to stand still. No one could call him Slow Joe those first hours; he operated in high gear for most of the morning. When he could not manage to stand still, John would drive Joe around the seaport again.

One of the things he'd never seen before were the Dyer boats sailing on the river. There are always little sailboats on the river because the seaport has a summer sailing camp.

The first time Joe spotted the bright colored sails moving on the water he snorted and trotted sideways down the road. John was patient and talked to Joe the whole time. Whenever the two horses passed, Duke would offer Joe little encouraging nickers.

Before long, Little Joe began to calm down. He realized he was getting a little tired and the noise of the old depot wagon didn't bother him anymore.

John started letting passengers on and they began giving tours.

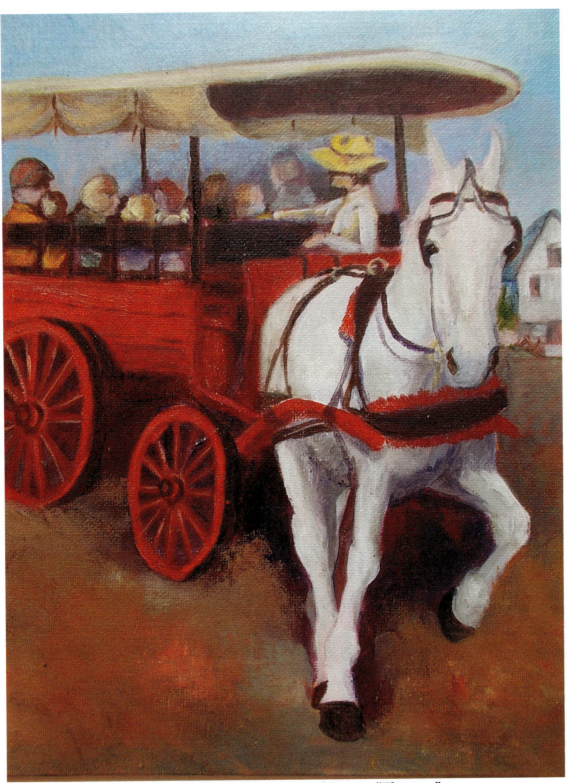

There was one word for Duke in harness and it was "Elegant".

The Depot Wagon

She's nice too

Joe was feeling pretty good about himself until they went back to the stable at the end of a long day. He spotted Zena looking over her stall door.

Joe realized she had probably seen his early performance when he was spooking all over the seaport. He was embarrassed and he could feel his nose turning pink again. He was thinking of something clever to say when Zena spoke first,

"I can't believe John made you pull that noisy old carriage on your first day at the seaport. There are enough distractions here to get used to without listening to that rattling bucket of bolts all day!"

Little Joe thought that was the nicest thing Zena could have said. He admitted the carriage had made him nervous at first.

"Now, Zena, that old depot wagon is a real piece of history." Duke said.

"A very NOISY piece of history!" Zena tossed her head. "You did really well on your first day, Joe. It took me a lot longer to settle down when I first started working here."

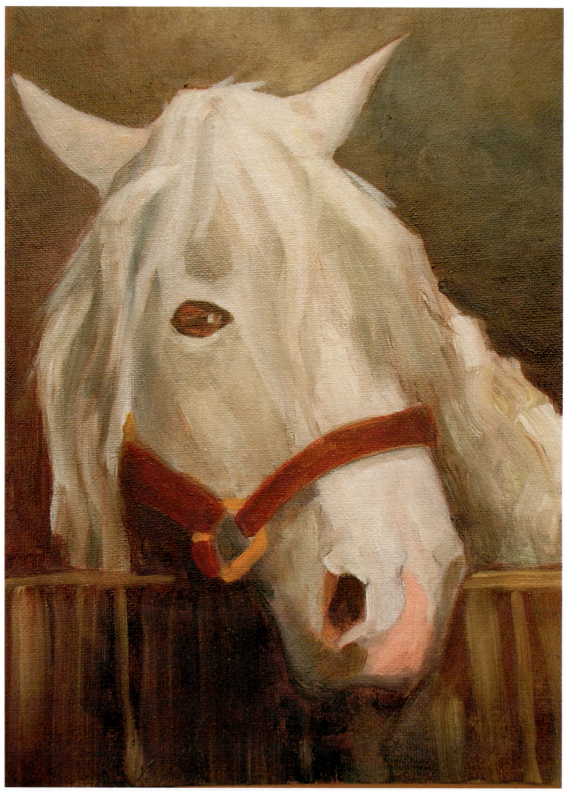
Joe's nose was turning pink again. Not only was Zena beautiful, she was nice too.

The Depot Wagon

Joe spotted the bright colored sails on the water.

Summer

The seaport got busier and busier over the summer. Joe got used to all the activity.

There were running children, crying children, yelling children and children who had never seen a live horse before. Cannons fired, hats that blew off and when it rained people opened umbrellas right under a poor horse's nose! There were wheel chairs and strollers and high-wheeled bicycles everyday. Joe learned to handle it all.

There were different carriage drivers on different days. Joe behaved well for them all; but some complained about him being a "Slow Joe". Joe worried, because he liked this job and he did not want to be sold again.

The summer went on and nothing changed. Joe did his work. The days could be long, but Joe had to agree the two days off was a really good idea. There did not seem to be a day missed in the apple and carrot department either.

Sometimes Duke would have to go to New York for an acting job. Zena and Joe were left to hold down the fort at the seaport. Joe missed his buddy, Duke, but he also liked spending more time with Zena.

The last big holiday of the summer is Labor Day weekend. The seaport is very crowded. After Labor Day, the seaport traffic slows way down because all the families have to get their children back to school.

It was at this time of year a new driver named Marty came to work for John. She began training with driver Amy who would soon have to go back to teaching school. Marty had worked with horses all her life but the Percherons were the biggest she had ever worked around.

Sometimes she'd get the giggles while brushing Duke because she couldn't reach the middle of his back. Duke thought it was pretty funny too. He knew she'd see the dirt she missed the minute she climbed up in the carriage seat and have to climb back down and brush again.

Marty and Joe became fast friends. Joe was the right size for her. She liked driving Joe on tours because he did walk slowly and that gave her plenty of time to talk. She appreciated Joe's sense of humor and they shared many a good horselaugh.

The rule for visiting the horses at the carriage stand is to pat the horses on their side and to stay away from their head. The reason for the rule is Percherons have very large heads weighing one hundred fifty pounds or more. Hundreds of people come through the seaport and even the best natured horse could become annoyed with hundreds pats on their nose and face.

Marty often had to remind visitors that Joe loved inspecting ladies hand bags and he was more thorough than airport security. He also knew that lunch bags might contain apples or carrots.

On one occasion a lady (who had a horse of her own at home) thought Joe was so cute, she kept kissing him on the nose. Marty kept politely asking the woman to please pat Joe's side instead. The woman kept right on kissing Joe's nose. The woman said,

"Oh, it's alright, I KNOW ALL ABOUT HORSES! I have a horse of my own."

Marty kept politely asking the woman to please stop but she also noticed that Joe moved over slightly to the right with each kiss. She realized that after a few steps Little Joe had maneuvered the woman in perfect alignment with his water barrel!

Then Marty said,

"Madam, I know you have a horse of your own and love horses dearly but I must warn you Joe has moved you to a spot where there is a LARGE FULL WATER BARREL DIRECTLY BEHIND YOU! I'm not sure what Joe has planned."

"Oh dear! You are quite the character Little Joe!" the woman laughed. "You are not as innocent as you look."

Joe was slightly disappointed that his little prank was spoiled but it didn't matter as everyone had a good laugh.

Joe got used to all the activity.

Autumn

Autumn can be a good time for the horses. Seaport weekends are still busy but there are not so many trips around the seaport on the weekdays and Little Joe could enjoy the occasional nap under the tree at the carriage stand.

When the weather turns cold, windy and rainy in the late fall the horses go back to the farm for a little vacation. It was around this time Joe learned he and Zena would be teammates for Lantern Light Tours at Christmas time.

John had them practice working in a team back at the farm. Sometimes Joe had to trot to keep up with Zena's long legs when they went around a corner. But he was determined to keep up and do the best job he could. Working with Zena in a team was a dream come true for Joe.

Joe and Zena now shared the pasture with the team of Loretta and Casper. It was nice to get to know them. Casper was a bit silly. Joe did not understand why Casper enjoyed rubbing his mane on a tree so much. Casper seemed to like his mane short and brush like. Joe couldn't help but laugh every time Loretta would roll her eyes and say,

"You look like a punk rocker!"

The Omnibus

Lantern Light Tours

Christmastime was fast approaching and the horses were ready to start working Lantern Light Tours.

Joe had asked a lot of questions about the job they were expected to do. As always Duke reassured him, he would do just fine. Duke was retired from doing the Lantern Light event but he had done it for many years.

Joe learned that Lantern Light Tours was a Christmas play. Actors in historical dress with lanterns would guide groups of visitors to different seaport buildings where more actors would tell the seaport's Christmas story. Humans seemed to enjoy this sort of thing. In fact many families make Lantern Light a Christmas tradition and come back year after year.

The day came for them to go back to the seaport. As always, Joe went where he was led and followed John and Zena on to the trailer. Casper and Loretta were loaded on the trailer next. They chatted and ate their hay on the journey back to the seaport.

They arrived late afternoon and the people waiting for them went straight to work grooming the horses. Next they were harnessed and as the sun was setting the pairs were hitched to the carriages. Joe and Zena were hooked to the big trolley carriage. Casper and Loretta were hooked to the tall Omnibus.

Each carriage has a human team, one driver and two footmen. One footman helps the driver with the horses and one helps passengers to board the carriage.

Dawn, Marty and Doug are on the Trolley and Katelyn, John and Nick on the Omnibus. Doug and John usually act as the spare drivers, in case Dawn or Katelyn would need a break during the long cold night.

By the time everyone was in place it was dark. The seaport's only lights were lanterns along the streets and walkways.

The horses patiently waited at the carriage stand. The first group of visitors was led to the trolley. The footman greeted the lady dressed in beautiful Victorian costume as he helped the passengers on.

"Merry Christmas!"

The first part of the Christmas story began as Zena and Joe pulled the trolley along. Throughout the night Zena and Joe worked side-by-side taking passengers to their destination.

Their team driver, Dawn, praised them often for the good job they were doing, even though she sometimes reminded Joe to keep up with Zena on the corners.

Joe was thinking how lucky he was. He had found his place in the world by following his mothers' advice.

"Be good and go where you are led."

Not only were he and Zena great teammates. Joe realized he was part of the bigger Lantern Light Tours team with Zena, Loretta, Casper, the drivers and the footmen. Back at John's farm there were more horses, more teammates. Little Joe thought to himself, it was more than a team. He was an important member of his new family. Joe felt happier than he had ever been.

The snow began to gently fall and cover the ground. Snowflakes stuck in the horses' manes and on their whiskers.

Someone passing on the street said,

"Look at the horses! They look like a perfect Christmas card!"

Joe said to Zena,

"We do look good together."

"Yes we do, Joe, yes we do."

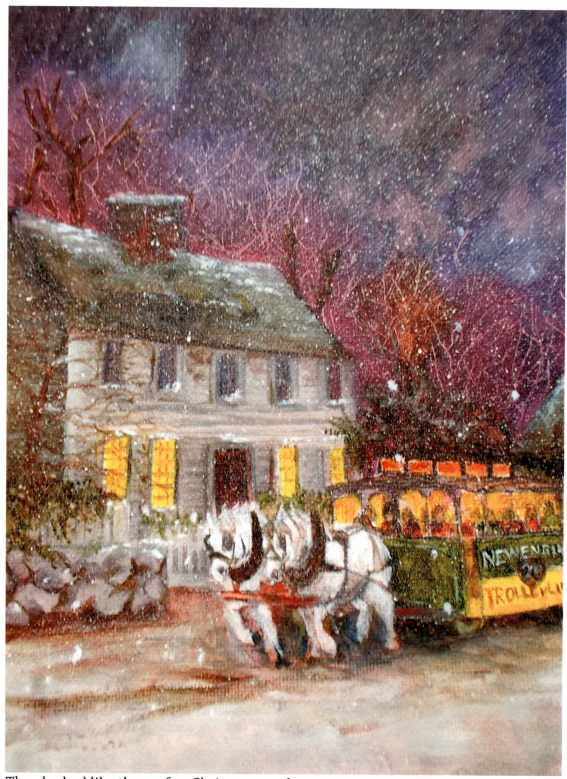

They looked like the perfect Christmas card.

Afterword

Anyone who thinks that horses cannot speak simply hasn't listened close enough. Every horse has a story and they know more about humans than they are given credit for.

The author met Joe several years ago and he has taught her much about the art of slowing down and enjoying life. She has learned from Little Joe it is best to go where one is led. Work hard when necessary but when business is slow there is nothing wrong with a short nap at the carriage stand.

Little Joe, Duke, Zena, Loretta, and Casper are very real horses that work at the Mystic Seaport, in Mystic, Ct.
During the off-season, the horses live happily with John Allegra and all the other horses at Allegra Farms in East Haddam, Ct.

Duke still enjoys listening carefully to human conversation on movie sets and elsewhere. He could write his own history book and continues to mentor young horses. (The author is convinced that if Duke could talk she would be out of a job!)

Little Joe and Zena are still teammates, and he sometimes works as the center horse in a three-horse team with Loretta and Casper. He has high hopes to follow in Duke's hoof prints and pursue an acting career and has already landed some spots in TV commercials.

All the horses agree,

"Best of all there are no plows!"

Made in the USA
Charleston, SC
16 July 2014